Twenty Poems by St. John of the Cross

# Twenty Poems by St. John of the Cross
by St. John of the Cross

Start Publishing PD LLC
Copyright © 2024 by Start Publishing PD LLC

All rights reserved, including the right to reproduce this book or portions thereof in any form whatsoever.

Start Publishing PD is a registered trademark of Start Publishing PD LLC
Manufactured in the United States of America

Cover art: Shutterstock/Taisiya Kozorez

Cover design: Jennifer Do

10 9 8 7 6 5 4 3 2 1

ISBN 979-8-8809-2419-6

# Table of Contents

His Heart an Open Wound. . . . . . . . . . . . . . . . . . . . . . . . . . . . . . 6
Trinity. . . . . . . . . . . . . . . . . . . . . . . . . . . . . . . . . . . . . . . . . . . . . . 7
Within the Trinity. . . . . . . . . . . . . . . . . . . . . . . . . . . . . . . . . . . . 9
By the Waters of Babylon. . . . . . . . . . . . . . . . . . . . . . . . . . . . . 10
Song of the Soul That Rejoices in Knowing God Through Faith. . . . . . . 12
The Dark Night. . . . . . . . . . . . . . . . . . . . . . . . . . . . . . . . . . . . . 13
The Living Flame of Love. . . . . . . . . . . . . . . . . . . . . . . . . . . . . 15
Stanzas Concerning an Ecstasy Experienced in High Contemplation. . . 16
Stanzas of the Soul That Suffers with Longing to See God. . . . . . . . . 19
Stanzas Given a Spiritual Meaning. . . . . . . . . . . . . . . . . . . . . . 21
A Gloss (With Spiritual Meaning). . . . . . . . . . . . . . . . . . . . . . 32
Full of Hope I Climbed the Day. . . . . . . . . . . . . . . . . . . . . . . . 36
I Came into the Unknown. . . . . . . . . . . . . . . . . . . . . . . . . . . . 38
I Live Yet Do Not Live in Me. . . . . . . . . . . . . . . . . . . . . . . . . . 40
Love's Living Flame. . . . . . . . . . . . . . . . . . . . . . . . . . . . . . . . . 42
The Fountain. . . . . . . . . . . . . . . . . . . . . . . . . . . . . . . . . . . . . . 43
The Sum of Perfection. . . . . . . . . . . . . . . . . . . . . . . . . . . . . . . 45
Without a Place and with a Place. . . . . . . . . . . . . . . . . . . . . . . 46
On the Communion of the Three Persons. . . . . . . . . . . . . . . . 48
A Spiritual Canticle of the Soul and the Bridegroom Christ. . . . . . . . . 50

# His Heart an Open Wound
## Stanzas Applied Spiritually to Christ and the Soul.

A lone young shepherd lived in pain
withdrawn from pleasure and contentment,
his thoughts fixed on a shepherd-girl
his heart an open wound with love.

He weeps, but not from the wound of love,
there is no pain in such affliction,
even though the heart is pierced;
he weeps in knowing he's been forgotten.

That one thought: his shining one
has forgotten him, is such great pain
that he bows to brutal handling in a foreign land,
his heart an open wound with love.

The shepherd says: I pity the one
who draws herself back from my love,
and does not seek the joy of my presence
though my heart is an open wound with love for her.

After a long time he climbed a tree,
and spread his shining arms,
and hung by them, and died,
his heart an open wound with love.

# Trinity

**Romance on the Gospel Text Regarding the Blessed Trinity.**

In the beginning the Word
was; he lived in God
and possessed in him
his infinite happiness.
That same Word was God,
who is the Beginning;
he was in the beginning
and had no beginning.
He was himself the Beginning
and therefore had no beginning!
The Word is called Son;
he was born of the Beginning
who had always conceived him,
and was always conceiving him,
giving of his substance always,
yet always possessing it.
And thus the glory of the Son
was the Father's glory,
and the Father possessed
all his glory in the Son.
As the lover in the beloved
each lived in the other,
and the Love that unites them
is one with them,
their equal, excellent as
the One and the Other:
Three Persons, and one Beloved
among all three.
One love in them all

makes of them one Lover,
and the Lover is the Beloved
in whom each one lives.
For the being that the three possess
each of them possesses,
and each of them loves
him who bears this being.
Each one is this being,
which alone unites them,
binding them deeply,
one beyond words.
Thus it is a boundless
Love that unites them,
for the three have one love
which is their essence;
and the more love is one
the more it is love.

# Within the Trinity
## On the Communication among the Three Persons.

In that immense love
proceeding from the two
the Father spoke words
of great affection to the Son,
words of such profound delight
that no one understood them;
they were meant for the Son,
and he alone rejoiced in them.
What he heard
was this:
"My Son, only your
company contents me,
and when something pleases me
I love that thing in you;
whoever resembles you most
satisfies me most,
and whoever is like you in nothing
will find nothing in me.
I am pleased with you alone,
O life of my life!
You are the light of my light,
you are my wisdom,
the image of my substance
in whom I am well pleased.
My Son, I will give myself
to him who loves you
and I will love him
with the same love I have for you,
because he has loved
you whom I love so."

# By the Waters of Babylon
## A Romance on the Psal

By the rivers
of Babylon
I sat down weeping,
there on the ground.
And remembering you,
0 Zion, whom I loved,
in that sweet memory
I wept even more.
I took off my feast-day clothes
and put on my working ones;
I hung on the green willows
all the joy I had in song,
putting it aside for that
which I hoped for in you.
There love wounded me
and took away my heart.
I begged love to kill me
since it had so wounded me;
I threw myself in its fire
knowing it burned,
excusing now the young bird
that would die in the fire.
I was dying in myself,
breathing in you alone.
I died within myself for you
and for you I revived,
because the memory of you
gave life and took it away.
The strangers among whom
I was captive rejoiced;
they asked me to sing
what I sang in Zion:
Sing us a song from Zion,

let's hear how it sounds.
I said: How can I sing,
in a strange land where I weep
for Zion, sing of the happiness
that I had there?
I would be forgetting her
if I rejoiced in a strange land.
May the tongue I speak with
cling to my palate if I forget you
in this land where I am.
Zion, by the green branches
Babylon holds out to me,
may my right hand be forgotten
(that I so loved when home in you)
if I do not remember you,
my greatest joy,
or celebrate one feast-day,
or feast at all without you.
O Daughter of Babylon,
miserable and wretched!
Blessed is he
in whom I have trusted,
for he will punish you
as you have me;
and he will gather his little ones
and me, who wept because of
you,
at the rock who is Christ
for whom I abandoned you.

# Song of the Soul That Rejoices in Knowing God Through Faith.

For I know well the spring that flows and runs,
although it is night.
That eternal spring is hidden, for I know well where it has its rise,
although it is night.

I do not know its origin, nor has it one,
but I know that every origin has come from it,
although it is night.

I know that nothing else is so beautiful,
and that the heavens and the earth drink there,
although it is night.

I know well that it is bottomless
and no one is able to cross it,
although it is night.

Its clarity is never darkened,
and I know that every light has
come from it,
although it is night.

# The Dark Night
**Songs of the Soul That Rejoices in Having Reached the High State of Perfection, Which Is Union with God, by the Path of Spiritual Negation.**

One dark night,
fired with love's urgent longings
- ah, the sheer grace! -
I went out unseen,
my house being now all stilled.

In darkness, and secure,
by the secret ladder, disguised,
ah, the sheer grace! -
in darkness and concealment,
my house being now all stilled.

On that glad night
in secret, for no one saw me,
nor did I look at anything
with no other light or guide
than the one that burned in my heart.

This guided me
more surely than the light of noon
to where he was awaiting me
- him I knew so well -
there in a place where no one appeared.

O guiding night!
O night more lovely than the dawn!
O night that has united

the Lover with his beloved,
transforming the beloved in her Lover.

Upon my flowering breast,
which I kept wholly for him alone,
there he lay sleeping,
and I caressing him
there in a breeze from the fanning cedars.

When the breeze blew from the turret,
as I parted his hair,
it wounded my neck
with its gentle hand,
suspending all my senses.

I abandoned and forgot myself,
laying my face on my Beloved;
all things ceased; I went out from myself,
leaving my cares
forgotten among the lilies.

# The Living Flame Of Love
## Songs of the Soul in the Intimate Communication of Loving Union with God.

O living flame of love
that tenderly wounds my soul
in its deepest center! Since
now you are not oppressive,
now consummate! if it be your will:
tear through the veil of this sweet encounter!

O sweet cautery,
O delightful wound!
O gentle hand! O delicate touch
that tastes of eternal life
and pays every debt!
In killing you changed death to life.

O lamps of fire!
in whose splendors
the deep caverns of feeling,
once obscure and blind,
now give forth, so rarely, so exquisitely,
both warmth and light to their Beloved.

How gently and lovingly
you wake in my heart,
where in secret you dwell alone;
and in your sweet breathing,
filled with good and glory,
how tenderly you swell my heart with love.

# Stanzas Concerning an Ecstasy Experienced in High Contemplation

I entered into unknowing,
and there I remained unknowing
transcending all knowledge.

I entered into unknowing,
yet when I saw myself there,
without knowing where I was,
I understood great things;
I will not say what I felt
for I remained in unknowing
transcending all knowledge.

That perfect knowledge
was of peace and holiness
held at no remove
in profound solitude;
it was something so secret
that I was left stammering,
transcending all knowledge.

I was so 'whelmed,
so absorbed and withdrawn,
that my senses were left
deprived of all their sensing,
and my spirit was given
an understanding while not understanding,
transcending all knowledge.

He who truly arrives there

cuts free from himself;
all that he knew before
now seems worthless,
and his knowledge so soars
that he is left in unknowing
transcending all knowledge.

The higher he ascends
the less he understands,
because the cloud is dark
which lit up the night;
whoever knows this
remains always in unknowing
transcending all knowledge.

This knowledge in unknowing
is so overwhelming
that wise men disputing
can never overthrow it,
for their knowledge does not reach
to the understanding of not understanding,
transcending all knowledge.

And this supreme knowledge
is so exalted
that no power of man or learning
can grasp it;
he who masters himself
will, with knowledge in
unknowing,
always be transcending.

And if you should want to hear:
this highest knowledge lies
in the loftiest sense
of the essence of God;
this is a work of his mercy,
to leave one without
understanding,

transcending all knowledge.

# Stanzas of the Soul That Suffers with Longing to See God.

I live, but not in myself,
and I have such hope
that I die because I do not die.

I no longer live within myself
and I cannot live without God,
for having neither him nor myself
what will life be?
It will be a thousand deaths,
longing for my true life
and dying because I do not die.

This life that I live
is no life at all,
and so I die continually
until I live with you;
hear me, my God:
I do not desire this life,
I am dying because I do not die.

When I am away from you
what life can I have
except to endure
the bitterest death known?
I pity myself,
for I go on and on living,
dying because I do not die.

A fish that leaves the water

has this relief:
the dying it endures
ends at last in death.
What death can equal my pitiable life?
For the longer I live, the more drawn out is my dying.

When I try to find relief
seeing you in the Sacrament,
I find this greater sorrow:
I cannot enjoy you wholly.
All things are affliction
since I do not see you as I desire,
and I die because I do not die.

And if I rejoice, Lord,
in the hope of seeing you,
yet seeing I can lose you
doubles my sorrow.
Living in such fear
and hoping as I hope,
I die because I do not die.

Lift me from this death,
my God, and give me life;
do not hold me bound
with these bonds so strong;
see how I long to see you;
my wretchedness is so complete
that I die because I do not die.

I will cry out for death
and mourn my living
while I am held here
for my sins.
O my God, when will it be
that I can truly say:
now I live because I do not die?

# Stanzas Given a Spiritual Meaning.

I went out seeking love,
and with unfaltering hope
I flew so high, so high,
that I overtook the prey.

That I might take the prey
of this adventuring in God
I had to fly so high
that I was lost from sight;
and though in this adventure
I faltered in my flight,
yet love had already flown so high
that I took the prey.

When I ascended higher
my vision was dazzled,
and the most difficult conquest
came about in darkness;
but since I was seeking love
the leap I made was blind and dark,
and I rose so high, so high,
that I took the prey.

The higher I ascended
in this seeking so lofty
the lower and more subdued
and abased I became.
I said: No one can overtake it!
And sank, ah, so low,
that I was so high, so high,

that I took the prey.

In a wonderful way
my one flight surpassed a
thousand,
for the hope of heaven
attains as much as it hopes for;
this seeking is my only hope,
and in hoping, I made no mistake,
because I flew so high, so high,
that I took the prey.

# Stanzas Applied Spiritually to Christ and the Soul

A lone young shepherd lived in pain
withdrawn from pleasure and contentment,
his thoughts fixed on a
shepherd-girl
his heart an open wound with love.

He weeps, but not from the wound of love,
there is no pain in such affliction,
even though the heart is pierced;
he weeps in knowing he's been forgotten.

That one thought: his shining one
has forgotten him, is such great pain
that he bows to brutal handling in a foreign land,
his heart an open wound with love.

The shepherd says: I pity the one
who draws herself back from my love,
and does not seek the joy of my presence,
though my heart is an open wound with love for her.

After a long time he climbed a tree,
and spread his shining arms,
and hung by them, and died,

# On the Communication Among the Three Persons.

In that immense love
proceeding from the two
the Father spoke words
of great affection to the Son,
words of such profound delight
that no one understood them;
they were meant for the Son,
and he alone rejoiced in them.

What he heard
was this:
"My Son, only your
company contents me,
and when something pleases me
I love that thing in you;
whoever resembles you most
satisfies me most,
and whoever is like you in nothing
will find nothing in me.
I am pleased with you alone,
O life of my life!
You are the light of my light,
you are my wisdom,
the image of my substance
in whom I am well pleased.
My Son, I will give myself
to him who loves you
and I will love him
with the same love I have for you,

because he has loved
you whom I love so."

On creation.
"My Son, I wish to give you
a bride who will love you.
Because of you she will deserve
to share our company,
and eat at our table,
the same bread I eat,
that she may know the good
I have in such a Son;
and rejoice with me
in your grace and fullness."
"I am very grateful,"
the Son answered;
"I will show my brightness
to the bride you give me,
so that by it she may see
how great my Father is,
and how I have received
my being from your being.
I will hold her in my arms
and she will burn with your love,
and with eternal delight
she will exalt your goodness."
"Let it be done, then," said the Father,
for your love has deserved it.
And by these words
the world was created,
a palace for the bride
made with great wisdom
and divided into rooms,
one above, the other below.
The lower was furnished
with infinite variety,
while the higher was made
beautiful
with marvelous jewels,

that the bride might know
the Bridegroom she had.
The orders of angels
were placed in the higher,
but humanity was given
the lower place,
for it was, in its being,
a lesser thing.
And though beings and places
were divided in this way,
yet all form one,
who is called the bride;
for love of the same Bridegroom
made one bride of them.
Those higher ones possessed
the Bridegroom in gladness;
the lower in hope, founded
on the faith that he infused in them,
telling them that one day
he would exalt them,
and that he would lift them
up from their lowness
so that no one
could mock it any more;
for he would make himself
wholly like them,
and he would come to them
and dwell with them;
and God would be man
and man would be God,
and he would walk with them
and eat and drink with them;
and he himself would be
with them continually
until the consummation
of this world,
when, joined, they would rejoice
in eternal song;
for he was the Head

of this bride of his
to whom all the members
of the just would be joined,
who form the body of the bride.
He would take her
tenderly in his arms
and there give her his love;
and when they were thus one,
he would lift her to the Father
where God's very joy
would be her joy.
For as the Father and the Son
and he who proceeds from them
live in one another,
so it would be with the bride;
for, taken wholly into God,
she will live the life of God.
By this bright hope
which came to them from above,
their wearying labors
were lightened;
but the drawn-out waiting
and their growing desire
to rejoice with their Bridegroom
wore on them continually.
So, with prayers
and sighs and suffering,
with tears and moanings
they asked night and day
that now he would determine
to grant them his company.
Some said: "If only
this joy would come in my time!"
Others: "Come, Lord,
send him whom you will send!"
And others: "Oh, if only these heavens
would break, and with my own eyes
I could see him descending;
then I would stop my crying out."

"Oh, clouds, rain down from your height,
earth needs you,
and let the earth open,
which has borne us thorns;
let it bring forth that flower
that would be its flowering."
Others said: "What gladness
for him who is living then,
who will be able to see God
with his own eyes,
and touch him with his hand
and walk with him
and enjoy the mysteries
which he will then ordain."
In these and other prayers
a long time had passed;
but in the later years
their fervor swelled and grew
when the aged Simeon
burned with longing,
and begged God that he
might see this day.
And so the Holy Spirit
answering the good old man
gave him his word
that he would not see death
until he saw Life
descending from the heights,
until he took God himself
into his own hands
and holding him in his arms,
pressed him to himself.

The Incarnation
Now that the time had come
when it would be good
to ransom the bride
serving under the hard yoke
of that law

which Moses had given her,
the Father, with tender love,
spoke in this way:
"Now you see, Son, that your bride
was made in your image,
and so far as she is like you
she will suit you well;
yet she is different, in her flesh,
which your simple being does not have.
In perfect love
this law holds:
that the lover become
like the one he loves;
for the greater their likeness
the greater their delight.
Surely your bride's delight
would greatly increase
were she to see you like her,
in her own flesh."
"My will is yours,"
the Son replied,
"and my glory is
that your will be mine.
This is fitting, Father,
what you, the Most High, say;
for in this way
your goodness will be more
evident,
your great power will be seen
and your justice and wisdom.
I will go and tell the world,
spreading the word
of your beauty and sweetness
and of your sovereignty.
I will go seek my bride
and take upon myself
her weariness and labors
in which she suffers so;
and that she may have life,

I will die for her,
and lifting her out of that deep,
I will restore her to you."
Then he called
the archangel Gabriel
and sent him to
the virgin Mary,
at whose consent
the mystery was wrought,
in whom the Trinity
clothed the Word with flesh.
and though Three work this,
it is wrought in the One;
and the Word lived incarnate
in the womb of Mary.
And he who had only a Father
now had a Mother too,
but she was not like others
who conceive by man.
From her own flesh
he received his flesh,
so he is called
Son of God and of man.

The Birth
When the time had come
for him to be born,
he went forth like the
bridegroom
from his bridal chamber,
embracing his bride,
holding her in his arms,
whom the gracious Mother
laid in a manger
among some animals
that were there at that time.
Men sang songs
and angels melodies
celebrating the marriage

of Two such as these.
But God there in the manger
cried and moaned;
and these tears were jewels
the bride brought to the
wedding.
The Mother gazed in sheer wonder
on such an exchange:
in God, man's weeping,
and in man, gladness,
to the one and the other
things usually so strange.
Finis

# A Gloss (With Spiritual Meaning)

Without support yet with support,
living without light, in darkness,
I am wholly being consumed. 1. My soul is disentangled
from every created thing
and lifted above itself
in a life of gladness
supported only in God.
So now it can be said
that I most value this:
My soul now sees itself
without support yet with support.

And though I suffer darknesses
in this mortal life,
that is not so hard a thing;
for even if I have no light
I have the life of heaven.
For the blinder love is
the more it gives such life,
holding the soul surrendered,
living without light in darkness.

After I have known it
love works so in me
that whether things go well or badly
love turns them to one sweetness
transforming the soul in itself.
And so in its delighting flame
which I am feeling within me,
swiftly, with nothing spared,

I am wholly being consumed.

A Gloss
Not for all of beauty
will I ever lose myself,
but for I-don't-know-what
which is so gladly gained.

Delight in the world's good things
at the very most
can only tire the appetite
and spoil the palate;
and so, not for all of sweetness
will I ever lose myself,
but for I-don't-know-what
which is so gladly found.

The generous heart
never delays with easy things
but eagerly goes on
to things more difficult.
Nothing satisfies it,
and its faith ascends so high
that it tastes I-don't-know-what
which is so gladly found.

He who is sick with love,
whom God himself has touched,
finds his tastes so changed
that they fall away
like a fevered man's
who loathes any food he sees
and desires I-don't know-what
which is so gladly found.

Do not wonder
that the taste should be left like this,
for the cause of this sickness
differs from all others;

and so he is withdrawn
from all creatures,
and tastes I-don't-know-what
which is so gladly found.

For when once the will
is touched by God himself,
it cannot find contentment
except in the Divinity;
but since his Beauty is open
to faith alone, the will
tastes him in I-don't-know-what
which is so gladly found.

Tell me, then, would you pity
a person so in love,
who takes no delight
in all creation;
alone, mind empty of form and figure,
finding no support or foothold,
he tastes there I-don't-know-what
which is so gladly found.

Do not think that he who lives
the so-precious inner life
finds joy and gladness
in the sweetness of the earth;
but there beyond all beauty
and what is and will be and was,
he tastes I-don't-know-what
which is so gladly found.

Whoever seeks to advance
takes much more care
in what he has yet to gain
than in what he has already gained;
and so I will always tend
toward greater heights;
beyond all things, to I-don't-know- what

which is so gladly found.

I will never lose myself
for that which the senses
can take in here,
nor for all the mind can hold,
no matter how lofty,
nor for grace or beauty,
but only for I-don't-know-what
which is so gladly found.

Christmas Refrain
The Virgin, weighed
with the Word of God,
comes down the road:
if only you'll shelter her.

The Sum of Perfection
Forgetfulness of created things,
remembrance of the Creator,
attention turned toward inward things,
and loving the Beloved.

# Full of Hope I Climbed the Day

Full of hope I climbed the day
while hunting the game of love,
and soared so high, high above
that at last caught my prey.

In order to seize the game
— the divine love in the sky —
I had to fly so high, high
I floated unseen and became
lost in that dangerous day;
and so my flight fell short of
height — yet so high was my love
that I at last caught my prey.

Dazzled and stunned by light
as I rose nearer the sun,
my greatest conquest was won
in the very black of night.
Yet since love opened my way
I leapt dark, blindly above
and was so high, near my love,
that at last I caught my prey.

In this most exalted quest
the higher I began to soar
the lower I felt — more sore
and broken and depressed.
I said: None can seize the prey!
and groveled so low, so low
that high, higher did I go,

and at last I caught my prey.

By strange reckoning I saw
a thousand flights in one flight;
for hope of heavenly light
is achieved by hoping now.
I hoped only for this way
and was right to wait for love,
and climbed so high, high above
that at last I caught my prey.

# I Came into the Unknown

I came into the unknown
and stayed there unknowing
rising beyond all science.

I did not know the door
but when I found the way,
unknowing where I was,
I learned enormous things,
but what I felt I cannot say,
for I remained unknowing,
rising beyond all science.

It was the perfect realm
of holiness and peace.
In deepest solitude
I found the narrow way:
a secret giving such release
that I was stunned and stammering,
rising beyond all science.

I was so far inside,
so dazed and far away
my senses were released
from feelings of my own.
My mind had found a surer way:
a knowledge of unknowing,
rising beyond all science.

And he who does arrive
collapses as in sleep,

for all he knew before
now seems a lowly thing,
and so his knowledge grows so deep
that he remains unknowing,
rising beyond all science.

The higher he ascends
the darker is the wood;
it is the shadowy cloud
that clarified the night,
and so the one who understood
remains always unknowing,
rising beyond all science.

This knowledge by unknowing
is such a soaring force
that scholars argue long
but never leave the ground.
Their knowledge always fails the source:
to understand unknowing,
rising beyond all science.

This knowledge is supreme
crossing a blazing height;
though formal reason tries
it crumbles in the dark,
but one who would control the night
by knowledge of unknowing
will rise beyond all science.

And if you wish to hear:
the highest science leads
to an ecstatic feeling
of the most holy Being;
and from his mercy comes his deed:
to let us stay unknowing,
rising beyond all science.

# I Live Yet Do Not Live in Me

I live yet do not live in me,
am waiting as my life goes by,
and die because I do not die.

No longer do I live in me,
and without God I cannot live;
to him or me I cannot give
my self, so what can living be?
A thousand deaths my agony
waiting as my life goes by,
dying because I do not die.

This life I live alone I view
as robbery of life, and so
it is a constant death — with no
way out until I live with you.
God, hear me, what I say is true:
I do not want this life of mine,
and die because I do not die.

Being so removed from you I say
what kind of life can I have here
but death so ugly and severe
and worse than any form of pain?
I pity me — and yet my fate
is that I must keep up this lie,
and die because I do not die.

The fish taken out of the sea
is not without a consolation:

his dying is of brief duration
and ultimately brings relief.
Yet what convulsive death can be
as bad as my pathetic life?
The more I live the more I die.

When I begin to feel relief
on seeing you in the sacrament,
I sink in deeper discontent,
deprived of your sweet company.
Now everything compels my grief:
I want — yet can't — see you nearby,
and die because I do not die.

Although I find my pleasure, Sir,
in hope of someday seeing you,
I see that I can lose you too,
which makes my pain doubly severe,
and so I live in darkest fear,
and hope, wait as life goes by,
dying because I do not die.

Deliver me from death, my God,
and give me life; now you have wound
a rope about me; harshly bound
I ask you to release the cord.
See how I die to see you, Lord,
and I am shattered where I lie,
dying because I do not die.

My death will trigger tears in me,
and I shall mourn my life: a day
annihilated by the way
I fail and sin relentlessly.
O Father God, when will it be
that I can say without a lie:
I live because I do not die?

# Love's Living Flame

(Songs that the soul sings in her intimate union with God, her beloved Bridegroom.)
O Love's living flame,
Tenderly you wound
My soul's deepest center!
Since you no longer evade me,
Will you, please, at last conclude:
Rend the veil of this sweet encounter!

O cautery so tender!
O pampered wound!
O soft hand! O touch so delicately strange,
Tasting of eternal life
And canceling all debts!
Killing, death into life you change!

O lamps of fiery lure,
In whose shining transparence
The deep cavern of the senses,
Blind and obscure,
Warmth and light, with strange flares,
Gives with the lover's caresses!

How tame and loving
Your memory rises in my breast,
Where secretly only you live,
And in your fragrant breathing,
Full of goodness and grace,
How delicately in love you make me feel!

# The Fountain

How well I know that flowing spring
in black of night.

The eternal fountain is unseen.
How well I know where she has been
in black of night.

I do not know her origin.
None. Yet in her all things begin
in black of night.

I know that nothing is so fair
and earth and firmament drink there
in black of night.

I know that none can wade inside
to find her bright bottomless tide
in black of night.

Her shining never has a blur;
I know that all light comes from her
in black of night.

I know her streams converge and swell
and nourish people, skies and hell
in black of night.

The stream whose birth is in this source
I know has a gigantic force
in black of night.

The stream from but these two proceeds
yet neither one, I know, precedes
in black of night.

The eternal fountain is unseen
in living bread that gives us being
in black of night.

She calls on all mankind to start
to drink her water, though in dark,
for black is night.

O living fountain that I crave,
in bread of life I see her flame in black of night.

# The Sum of Perfection

Creation forgotten,
Creator only known,
Attention turned inward
In love with the Beloved alone.

# Without a Place and With a Place

Without a place and with a place
to rest — living darkly with no ray
of light — I burn my self away.

My soul — no longer bound — is free
from the creations of the world;
above itself it rises hurled
into a life of ecstasy,
leaning only on God. The world
will therefore clarify at last
what I esteem of highest grace:
my soul revealing it can rest
without a place and with a place.

Although I suffer a dark night
in mortal life, I also know
my agony is slight, for though
I am in darkness without light,
a clear heavenly life I know;
for love gives power to my life,
however black and blind my day,
to yield my soul, and free of strife
to rest — living darkly with no ray.

Love can perform a wondrous labor
which I have learned internally,
and all the good or bad in me
takes on a penetrating savor,
changing my soul so it can be
consumed in a delicious flame.

I feel it in me as a ray;
and quickly killing every trace
of light — I burn my self away.

# On the Communion of the Three Persons (from Romance on the Gospel)

Out of the vast love
born of them both,
the Father spoke to the Son
with words of celebration,

with words of such full delight
that none can know;
only the Son, only he took joy,
since they were breathed in his ear alone.

But here is what
can be understood:
— "Nothing, my Son, pleases me,
but your company.

"If something is sweet,
through you alone do I taste it.
The more of you I see in its reflection,
the wider my smile;

"What is unlike you,
has nothing of me.
In you alone is my delight,
life of my life!

"You are the fire of my fire,
my knowing;
the form of my substance,
in you am I well pleased.

"Whoever gives his love to you, my Son,
to him I give myself,
and him I fill
with the love I feel for you
just for making you beloved,
my Beloved."

# A Spiritual Canticle of the Soul and the Bridegroom Christ

**The Bride**
Where have You hidden Yourself,
And abandoned me in my groaning, O my Beloved?
You have fled like the hart,
Having wounded me.
I ran after You, crying; but You were gone.

O shepherds, you who go
Through the sheepcots up the hill,
If you shall see Him
Whom I love the most,
Tell Him I languish, suffer, and die.

In search of my Love
I will go over mountains and strands;
I will gather no flowers,
I will fear no wild beasts;
And pass by the mighty and the frontiers.

O groves and thickets
Planted by the hand of the Beloved;
O verdant meads
Enameled with flowers,
Tell me, has He passed by you?

**Answer of the Creatures**
A thousand graces diffusing
He passed through the groves in haste,
And merely regarding them
As He passed

Clothed them with His beauty.

**The Bride**
Oh! who can heal me?
Give me at once Yourself,
Send me no more
A messenger
Who cannot tell me what I wish.

All they who serve are telling me
Of Your unnumbered graces;
And all wound me more and more,
And something leaves me dying,
I know not what, of which they are darkly speaking.

But how you persevere, O life,
Not living where you live;
The arrows bring death
Which you receive
From your conceptions of the Beloved.

Why, after wounding
This heart, have You not healed it?
And why, after stealing it,
Have You thus abandoned it,
And not carried away the stolen prey?

Quench my troubles,
For no one else can soothe them;
And let my eyes behold You,
For You are their light,
And I will keep them for You alone.

Reveal Your presence,
And let the vision and Your beauty kill me,
Behold the malady
Of love is incurable
Except in Your presence and before Your face.

O crystal well!
Oh that on Your silvered surface
You would mirror forth at once
Those eyes desired
Which are outlined in my heart!

Turn them away, O my Beloved!
I am on the wing:
**The Bridegroom**
Return, My Dove!
The wounded hart
Looms on the hill
In the air of your flight and is refreshed.

My Beloved is the mountains,
The solitary wooded valleys,
The strange islands,
The roaring torrents,
The whisper of the amorous gales;

The tranquil night
At the approaches of the dawn,
The silent music,
The murmuring solitude,
The supper which revives, and enkindles love.

Catch us the foxes,
For our vineyard has flourished;
While of roses
We make a nosegay,
And let no one appear on the hill.

O killing north wind, cease!
Come, south wind, that awakens love!
Blow through my garden,
And let its odors flow,
And the Beloved shall feed among the flowers.

O nymphs of Judea!
While amid the flowers and the rose-trees
The amber sends forth its perfume,
Tarry in the suburbs,
And touch not our thresholds.

Hide yourself, O my Beloved!
Turn Your face to the mountains,
Do not speak,
But regard the companions
Of her who is traveling amidst strange islands.

**The Bridegroom**
Light-winged birds,
Lions, fawns, bounding does,
Mountains, valleys, strands,
Waters, winds, heat,
And the terrors that keep watch by night;

By the soft lyres
And the siren strains, I adjure you,
Let your fury cease,
And touch not the wall,
That the bride may sleep in greater security.

The bride has entered
The pleasant and desirable garden,
And there reposes to her heart's content;
Her neck reclining
On the sweet arms of the Beloved.

Beneath the apple-tree
There were you betrothed;
There I gave you My hand,
And you were redeemed
Where your mother was corrupted.

## The Bride

Our bed is of flowers
By dens of lions encompassed,
Hung with purple,
Made in peace,
And crowned with a thousand shields of gold.

In Your footsteps
The young ones run Your way;
At the touch of the fire
And by the spiced wine,
The divine balsam flows.

In the inner cellar
Of my Beloved have I drunk; and when I went forth
Over all the plain
I knew nothing,
And lost the flock I followed before.

There He gave me His breasts,
There He taught me the science full of sweetness.
And there I gave to Him
Myself without reserve;
There I promised to be His bride.

My soul is occupied,
And all my substance in His service;
Now I guard no flock,
Nor have I any other employment:
My sole occupation is love.

If, then, on the common land
I am no longer seen or found,
You will say that I am lost;
That, being enamored,
I lost myself; and yet was found.

Of emeralds, and of flowers

In the early morning gathered,
We will make the garlands,
Flowering in Your love,
And bound together with one hair of my head.

By that one hair
You have observed fluttering on my neck,
And on my neck regarded,
You were captivated;
And wounded by one of my eyes.

When You regarded me,
Your eyes imprinted in me Your grace:
For this You loved me again,
And thereby my eyes merited
To adore what in You they saw

Despise me not,
For if I was swarthy once
You can regard me now;
Since You have regarded me,
Grace and beauty have You given me.

**The Bridegroom**
The little white dove
Has returned to the ark with the bough;
And now the turtle-dove
Its desired mate
On the green banks has found.

In solitude she lived,
And in solitude built her nest;
And in solitude, alone
Has the Beloved guided her,
In solitude also wounded with love.

**The Bride**
Let us rejoice, O my Beloved!

Let us go forth to see ourselves in Your beauty,
To the mountain and the hill,
Where the pure water flows:
Let us enter into the heart of the thicket.

We shall go at once
To the deep caverns of the rock
Which are all secret,
There we shall enter in
And taste of the new wine of the pomegranate.

There you will show me
That which my soul desired;
And there You will give at once,
O You, my life!
That which You gave me the other day.

The breathing of the air,
The song of the sweet nightingale,
The grove and its beauty
In the serene night,
With the flame that consumes, and gives no pains.

None saw it;
Neither did Aminadab appear
The siege was intermitted,
And the cavalry dismounted
At the sight of the waters.

www.ingramcontent.com/pod-product-compliance
Lightning Source LLC
Chambersburg PA
CBHW031431040426
42444CB00006B/766